D0216664

Edition Bach-Archiv Leipzig

Hans-Joachim Schulze

Ey! How sweet the coffee tastes

Johann Sebastian Bach's Coffee Cantata in its time

Translated by Alfred Mann

EVANGELISCHE VERLAGSANSTALT
Leipzig

Illustrated by Christiane Knorr

Bibliographic information published by the
Deutsche Nationalbibliothek
The Deutsche Nationalbibliothek lists this publication in the
Deutsche Nationalbibliographie; detailed bibliographic data
are available on the Internet at http://dnb.dnb.de.

2nd edition 2016
© 2006 by Evangelische Verlagsanstalt GmbH · Leipzig
Printed in Germany · H 7048

This book is printed on ageing resistant paper.

All rights reserved
Typesetting: Ulrike Kollodzeiski, Leipzig
Cover: Ulrike Vetter, Leipzig
Printing and Binding: CPI books GmbH, Leck

ISBN 978-3-374-02365-3
www.eva-leipzig.de

From Coffee Bush to "Coffee Tree"

A good coffee must be as hot as the kisses of a girl on the first day, as sweet as her love on the third day, and as black as her mother's curses, when she finds out about it.

Old oriental wisdom of the Coffee House is said to have devised this fitting comparison. And even if the proverb is not genuine, at least it is a good fabrication – as good as the majority of reports from ancient and recent times about the origin and spread of the good – or bad – custom of the enjoyment of coffee.

During the period that the English call "Enlightenment", which literally means "illumination", the following story appeared in the *Great, Complete Universal Lexicon of all Sciences and Arts*, a huge encyclopedia published in Leipzig and in the neighboring city of Halle:

"The use of this drink is said to have been learned by humans from their animals in the following manner. A shepherd in Arabia or in the surrounding territory is said to have been guarding a herd of camels, or as some say, goats, in the mountains." One day he told a clergyman that the cattle had not slept the whole night, but rather had jumped around in the stall. Upon investigation, they discovered bushes with unknown fruit, from which the prior of the nearby monastery had a drink prepared.

After consuming the drink, he also "felt himself completely enlivened. He, therefore, recommended this drink to his clergymen, so that they would not sleep so much during the early morning services."

The "enlightened" lexicon author is not completely sure of the story, and so he cautiously does not name his source. When this coffee article appeared in 1733, the story was already half a century old. It probably dates back to the portentous year 1685.

In many respects the year 1685 was a year of

destiny for the market metropolis of Leipzig. In this year an eighth child was born to Johann Ambrosius Bach, the town musician of the distant city of Eisenach. This child answered to the name Johann Sebastian (when it was so inclined) and, decades later, for various reasons, gave the Leipzig city council, the church officials, the city musicians and the choir students many a headache. The year 1685 also saw the birth of the first Leipzig coffee house, "At the Arabic Coffee Tree," which still flourishes today.

Originally the "Coffee Tree" was located in a rear building belonging to the property on Hainstreet 1, but in 1556 it was separated from it, becoming an independent property. In 1603, through the error of a town clerk, this house received a licence for selling wine and beer, and,

near the end of the seventeenth century, it was Adam Heinrich Schütz, whose occupation was gold-plating, who set up billiard tables and began serving coffee. In 1716 his daughter married Johann Lehmann, who, after three years, left this world and also the "Coffee Tree" – and so the establishment was known for decades as "Lehmann's Widow." The painting that hung over the entrance – an oriental figure with all imaginable accessories – was said to have been a gift from August the Strong, who in 1694 enjoyed the good coffee (or as others would have it, the hostess). However, no historian has yet been found to confirm this.

Let's assume then that, with regard to the first public coffee house in Leipzig, at least the year 1685 can be accepted as fact. There is, however, an anecdote from the year 1637 in neighboring Merseburg indicating that Leipzigers had enjoyed coffee much earlier.

A merchant in Merseburg had received a quantity of coffee from a business associate in the Netherlands. No recipe for its preparation had been included, however. The wife of the merchant cooked the pleasantly exotic beans carefully in a meat broth and then served it to her guests, expecting praise. The guests, each according to his temperament and talents, cleverly avoided comment. Only the servant, who had tasted the broth, ventured to observe that it tasted like a mixture of boot-black and herring-pickle. Whether or not he came to this judgement from experience unfortunately cannot be determined. Demands by the good Merseburger grocer for remedy, especially sixteen coins for medication, were brusquely rejected by the thrifty merchant from Holland.

"I have sent samples to Leipzig and everyone there praised the drink. This proves that the people in Leipzig have a more delicate taste than you

vulgar Merseburgers." This was, of course, the end of the business relationship between the two merchants.

Needless to say, sending gifts without instructions in this way can often give rise to unclear or false ideas and, as a result, shake the foundations of whole business empires. But the dissemination of news at that time was limited; since there were few who were privileged to have seen foreign countries, the majority had to choose whether they wanted to believe everything that they were told or, to be on the safe side, believe nothing at all. This applied also to the peculiar science of coffee-drinking, which Leonhard Rauwolf of Augsburg brought back in the 1570s from his trip to the Orient:

"Among other good things the Moslems also have a beverage, which they love very much. It is called 'chaube'. They drink it from small clay or porcelain cups in small sips, so they don't burn their mouths. The beverage is black as ink, bitter as gall, and smells somewhat scorched. But they are completely wild about their blackish stomach elixir, which is also said to be very useful against various illnesses."

The belief in the use of coffee as a primary medication, though obviously considered a luxury, persisted for centuries. In a booklet entitled *Caffe- und The-[tea]-Logia or Short Advertisement and Description of These Beverages ... Drafted by a somewhat experienced coffee drinker: Published this year* (1690) includes the following "Legend of a Coffee-House":

He who has filled his stomach three or four days
or indeed a whole week
With wine or strong beer,
So that he is weak nigh unto death,
And nothing can be found
to dispel this evil,
[He] who is bound to his bed by [gall bladder] stones
and gout,
Who is racked with pain in his bowels and intestines;
For which he must have warm cloths applied
And must take care that he always remains warm.
[He] who caught something on the trip to France,
Who has brought back syphilis ["Rubinen" = ruby
coloured rash] from Italy,
Whose face has been attacked by blotches,
Of whom the pimples made an enemy.

All of them must at once use the coffee-beverage;
There is no better remedy on earth for them.
In addition they must smoke as much tobacco
as they themselves deem good;
Then all pain will completely disappear.
He who wants to put his virtue to the test,
He should drink himself full of wine early mornings,
As soon as he drinks coffee, all intoxication will
disappear
And he will be sober again,
no matter how drunk he was.

There was not a moment of doubt about the necessity for that type of drastic treatment. In the same year that the first German coffee-house opened in Hamburg, 1671, the Swedish Queen Christine said with disgust, "The Germans are dumb drunkards, their country is cold, foul smelling and barbaric. The Bishop of Salzburg is only popular because he drinks a barrel of wine daily."

But not everyone was so opinionated. Liselotte von der Pfalz, since 1671 sister-in-law of the "Sun King" Louis XIV and author of some blunt descriptions of court life, expressed a different viewpoint in Paris, which was the center of the continental coffee culture:

"I can tolerate neither tea nor coffee nor chocolate. On the other hand, a beer soup would taste good to me, but one cannot obtain that because the beer in France is worthless (1712)!

I cannot tolerate coffee, tea or chocolate, and cannot understand, what one sees in these things! A good meal of sauerkraut and smoked sausage is a meal for a king, and I can think of nothing better […] A cabbage soup with bacon is more to my

taste than all the sweet dainties, about which the Parisians are so passionate (1714).

I seldom eat breakfast, but when I do, I eat only a buttered bread. These foreign seasonings and spices are utterly detestable to me. I [...] am completely like the Germans, in food and drink only that tastes good to me that has our forefathers' stamp of approval (1716)."

"Our forefathers' stamp of approval" points to a time, chiefly from the fifteenth to the seventeenth century, in which the good beer, along with the somewhat less desirable second infusion, known as Konventbeer, or Kofent, became the main beverage in German territories. It was a beverage whose constant enjoyment created a type of corpulent individual, which is depicted on paintings and portraits of this era: Luther and Bach, Peter Vischer and Hans Sachs, Handel and Pirckheimer, Gustav Adolf and Henry VIII. Didn't Bach's own father, Johann Ambrosius Bach, who became town piper in Eisenach in 1671, take over the hereditary privilege of brewing the "housebeer" himself while he ordered the "Kofent" from the city brewery? Didn't the gymnasiasts [i.e., pupils of secondary school] in the Thuringian town of Arnstadt in May 1705 perform an operetta of which the twenty-year-old organist Johann Sebastian Bach must have been at least an eye- and ear-witness? Unfortunately only the text remains of the operetta, which was entitled "The Intelligence of the Authorities in the Regulation of Beer Brewing." Note carefully: beer brewing, not coffee brewing! Then, too, didn't Bach's cousin in Jena, Johann Nikolaus Bach, write a student farce entitled, "The Wine and Beer Town Crier of Jena?"

The supremacy of beer was nowhere attacked, let alone broken, and it is symptomatic that at an organ consecration in Halle in May 1716, in which Bach himself participated, considerable amounts of Löbejüner and Merseburger beer were consumed, along with Frankenwine, Rhinewine and "tobacco", but only three pots of coffee were served, which cost alltogether twelve pennies. The same situation occurred thirty years later in Naumburg on-the-Saale. At the consecration of the famous Hildebrandt organ, in which Bach and Gottfried Silbermann were doing the honors, "spirituous" drinks predominated considerably. Apart from beer, twenty-eight jugs of wine plus two jugs of red wine (at departure) were drunken, and only little money was spent "on coffee, Canasder tobacco, pipes."

However, even though it was not until around 1730 that the custom of coffee drinking began to spread slowly from the royal courts to the middle class, this development had already taken place approximately four decades before in the cosmopolitan trade cities of Hamburg and especially Leipzig. Even there, however, coffee lovers faced some obstacles at first.

The Coffeehouse –

Place of Vice or Erudition?

At the same time that, in Paris, the widowed Duchess of Orleans, Elizabeth Charlotte ("Liselotte von der Pfalz"), argued for beersoup and sauerkraut, there was starting a discussion about the coffeehouses, which had rapidly fallen into disrepute and about which now a decision had to be made. Intervention by order of the authorities had to take place, so that these establishments would no longer be regarded as "breeding places for immorality and light-heartedness". At its January meeting in 1697, the Leipzig council consequently ordered the councilmen and city rulers to visit the coffeehouses. Women of the street and rabble were arrested and, in certain cases of indecent behavior, punished with beatings and banishment from the city or with monetary penalties. Apparently these measures had no immediate outstanding success for, even in 1715, the *Ladies Lexicon* by the Leipzig notary and lawyer Gottlieb Siegmund Corvinus warned: "They are 'coffee hussies', these slovenly women who serve the male customers and grant them every possible request." Goethe's *Venetian Epigrams* of 1790 describe the same circumstances in somewhat plainer language and with other stabbing words:

You want to know what such dens are? This book of epigrams will serve you as a dictionary. They are dark houses in narrow alleys; the pretty one leads you to the coffee, and she shows what she can do, not you.

Exactly one century ago the *"Caffe- and The* [tea]-*Logia"* claimed to have observed similar conditions in England, Holland, and even in Italy: "In such places it is not uncommon that a wench dressed in men's clothing sometimes appears in the coffee houses or that the innkeeper keeps in house a gallant lady for the bodily pleasures of his guests."

It is not easy to reconcile the perceptions, reported at this same time by the Persians, that strong coffee proved to be an "excellent amorous antidote, or a cure for an inordinate desire for love."

Whether the coffee cooked in Leipzig had not attained the required strength, or whether the city council did not want to give its wise approval to such nursery tales, is not reported. At any rate, in 1716 an ordinance attempting to put a stop to the

deterioration of good manners without making a distinction between moral concepts and class differences was passed:

"Since, however, billiard games are generally also held in these coffee-houses, the fashionable coffee establishments here in Leipzig must comply with the following rules: 1) The presence and service of all female persons in coffee-houses, including those involved in the preparation of the beverage and its serving, no matter with what excuse it might occur, 2) as well as all dice and card games, including any other games of chance, with the exception of billiards, are strictly forbidden; infractions will result in penalties to the coffee-house. 3) No one will be permitted, on penalty of 20 Thaler, to remain in such coffee-houses after nine o'clock in the evening in winter and ten o'clock in summer, and these houses are not permitted to remain open after these hours. 4) The young men who are apprenticed to merchants and tradesmen will not be permitted to play billiards, 5) no excessively high stakes in the game of billiards are permitted, but rather a certain amount [...] according to the quality and condition [...]."

In cases of violation there were given penalties

of ten or twenty Thaler, and if done repeatedly the license was revoked. On behalf of the university and its own competence, an order of the Rector issued a warning against visits in coffee and tea houses, particularly against dancing, gambling, and conversation with disreputable women.

As always in such situations, higher authority seems to have found the right word at the right time. Very quickly Leipzig's coffee houses rid themselves of the curse of looseness and adapted themselves to prevailing civic values. A guidebook for the town published in 1725 could honestly state:

"The eight licensed public coffee houses provide entertainment for people of all rank, ladies and gentlemen from our local populations as well as strangers. Their fine reputation rests on their beautiful location and accommodations, as well as on the large assemblies that occur daily. Everyone attending them will find interesting reading or entertainment at billiard-tables or in reputable games, such as chess or dominos."

The *Great, Complete Universal Lexicon* of 1730 does not look upon this quite so positively. In its entry "a coffee tavern" it quotes fully the restrictions of the 1716 council order, and in an article with the titel "a coffee house" it does not suppress this broad hint:

"At some places they offer the opportunity for gambling and other prohibited entertainment, so that superiors and sovereigns should keep a watchful eye on them. At others they offer good and informed conversation, pleasant and useful acquaintances, current press or other matters valuable to everyone. In Holland or England no one needs to avoid coffee houses, be it lay people or people of the cloth."

Thus what Montesquieu wrote in his 1721 *Lettres Persanes* may have applied to the Leipzig coffee houses – at least to some of them:

"Coffee is very fashionable in Paris. In the houses where it is offered, it is so prepared that it lends inspiration to those who drink it – in leaving, one believes to have four times as much inspiration as upon having entered."

Abundant praise was given especially to the "Kaffeebaum" in 1744 by Friedrich Wilhelm Zachariä, by that time eighteen years old and later belonging to the "Bremer Beiträger". His comic hero saga *Der Renommist* (The Grandiloquent) elaborates upon the dapper Leipzig student and his ruffian Jena counterpart:

The entrance depicts forthwith
That this is a temple dedicated to the god of coffee.
An Arabian lies under a coffee tree,
And what is brought to him in bright of sweetened
froth,
Cooked from oriental beans sent from the Levant,
Is offered by a naked cupido who looks at him
smilingly.

More than two decades after this was written in Alexandrine verse, a clique of Leipzig students, "enjoying a delicious cake while gathering in the cabbage fields", hit on the idea of toasting in dithyrambic verses to the cakebaker who lived in the eastern surroundings of the town. Their point was in discrediting Professor Clodius and the grandiloquence of his imitations of Ramler's Odes. A house wall willingly allowed itself to be inscribed:

Oh, Hendel, whose fame spans North and South,
Hear the paean that rises to your ears!

Your genius creates unique cake,
Sought after by French and British.
The coffee's ocean that springs from you
Is sweeter than what flows from Hymettus.

The only sketch of the full poem (thrice this length) has unfortunately been lost, as has the sketch of its serious and very famous counterpart, which the author of this cakebaker hymn wrote on the wall of the hunting lodge on the Kickelhahn near Ilmenau in Thuringia in 1780.

Hendel's plum and apple cakes drew universal fame, but the quality of his coffee was also generally admired. Whether or not comparison with the honey that lent fame to Hymettus (the mountain near Athens) is appropriate may be left to future Goethe scholarship.

Not only Goethe, but Schiller also enjoyed the phenomenon of the Leipzig coffee house. The latter said in 1785: "My most pleasant diversion has always been to visit Richter's coffee house, where one is apt to meet just about half of Leipzig's society."

About the same time, a contemporary remarked:

"The coffee houses in Paris, the Hague, and Vienna, etc., are the most famous among those of Europe. So far as the splendor of trappings is concerned, the new Leipzig coffee house of Richter may lead them all. Here the most exquisite concerts are given at the time of the fair. Service and refreshments are superior, and the evening hours for many a visitor to the fair are enhanced."

Finally, the famous *Journal of Luxury and Fashion [Journal des Luxus und der Moden]* reads:

"Regular concerts have been unvaryingly held here for forty or more years. A musical society had gathered already in those days at Enoch Richter's whose name attained wide fame through his erstwhile coffee house (now unfortunately abolished). It offered weekly concerts, either there or in the garden, according to the season, which received special interest through their novelties [...] gentlemen in their later years will remember to have seen the dignified figure of Sebastian Bach conducting there in his incomparable spiritedness."

These remarks refer to the so-called "Romanus House", at the corner of Brühl and Katharinenstrasse, which the ambitious mayor Franz Conrad

Romanus had erected between 1701 and 1704. During the second half of the eighteenth century the well-known coffee house of Richter was located on the second floor of the building, which resembled a *palais* rather than an ordinary civic dwelling. Concerts were given there since the end of the Seven Years' War until the 1790s. It is unlikely, however, that Bach appeared there. Before 1750 Enoch Richter's café was located elsewhere: in a house at Katharinenstrasse 14, which had been built in 1717 (and fell victim to the war in 1943). It was a magnificent Baroque building with several large guest rooms on the second floor. This must be the building to which the news item of 1749 refers:

"Tomorrow evening at five o'clock the popular musical poem 'The power of music', will be repeated at Richter's coffee house upon the efforts of good friends – which we now make known to all unbiased connoisseurs of music."

And doubtless the following notice from a 1736 Leipzig music journal belongs to the same context,

"Both of the public musical Concerts or Assemblies that are held here weekly are still flour-

ishing steadily. The one is conducted by Mr.
Johann Sebastian Bach, Capellmeister to the
Court of Weissenfels and *Musik-Direktor* at St.
Thomas's and at St. Nicholas's in this city, and is
held, except during the Fair, once a week in Zimmermann's coffeehouse in the Catherine Street,
on Friday evenings from 8 to 10 o'clock; during
the Fair, however, twice a week, on Tuesdays and
Fridays, at the same hour. The other is conducted
by Mr. Johann Gottlieb Görner, *Musik-Direktor* at
St. Paul's and Organist at St. Thomas's. It is also
held once weekly, in the Schellhafer Hall in the

Closter-Gasse, Thursday evenings from 8 to 10 o'clock; during the Fair, however, twice weekly, namely, Mondays and Thursdays, at the same time.

The participants in these musical concerts are chiefly students here, and there are always good musicians among them, so that sometimes they become, as is known, famous virtuosos. Any musician is permitted to make himself publicly heard at these musical concerts, and most often, too, there are such listeners as know how to judge the qualities of an able musician." [translation from *The New Bach Reader*, pp. 185–86]

Without any doubt it was for the "Bach Collegium Musicum" with its weekly concerts "in Zimmermann's coffeehouse in the Catherine Street", during the warm season "at Zimmermann's garden", on Grimmischer Stein-Weg, that Johann Sebastian Bach wrote his "drama per musica" entitled "Schlendrian and his daughter Liesgen", which, as documented by 1754, went under the name of "Coffee Cantata".

Problems of Librettists

The libretto appeared in the year 1732 and was neither the only one nor the oldest of its kind in existence. In 1703 the French composer Nicolas Bernier had a cantata with the title "Le Caffé" printed in his *Troisième livre des cantates françoises*. Johann Gottfried Krause, a private tutor in Weissenfels, offered in his *First Bouquet of poetic flowers for joyous and mournful occasions, picked in leisurely hours at the pleasurable shores of the Saale river,* 1716, a cantata text under the title "Lob des Coffee." Krause's statement in the preface that he had taken "no formal course in poetry" is not hard to believe in view of the following sample:

Coffee, coffee is my life,
Coffee is the potion of the gods.
Without coffee I am ill.
Even the sweet juice of the vine
Is superseded by coffee.

...

For if I want to mount the hill of Pindus
And want to devise a poem,
I need only a cup of coffee,
And, should opportunity lend itself,
Smoke a pipe of tobacco with it,
Then I sense immediately
That the muses favor my pen.

Daniel Stoppe from Hirschberg in Silesia seems a little less philistine. After studies in Leipzig and Jena he lived for a long time in his hometown without steady employment, as a private tutor, before marrying into a grocer's business and thus becoming solvent. His poetry manifests a large range of themes and forms, ranging from the fairly crass wedding offering to the sacred cantata, from the likeness of French fables to the buffoonery in Silesian dialect. In addtition to emulating Gottsched, he copied Johann Christian Günther, a colleague from his region, as in his 1728 text for a "coffee cantata":

Just wait, you lazy veins!
My coffee will awaken and enliven you,
It will serve you well,
It will gladden your faint heart.
Snore away! You will soon awake.

It will change sluggish night to busy day.
Even when the clock shows almost midnight,
Even when sleep seems about to triumph,
Coffee emerges as the enemy.
It will rule the day.

As soon as it enters the stomach, the former flees from
the eyes.
...
Let restless spirits swarm about,
Quiet them with a dish of coffee,
And, lighting a pipe,
You will have anxiety disappear.
With its bubbles
The sugar's invasion
Will bid goodbye
To all worries,
Instantly ending their troubled raging.

The third in this confraternity of cantata authors is Bach's "house poet" Picander – his pseudonym for Christian Friedrich Henrici. Like Stoppe's, his career was at first beset with problems, which he managed with tutoring and occasional poetic work. Few people had so great a talent as he for appropriating the ideas of others and refashioning them – in this way precluding the charge of plagiarism. Adroitness, adaptility and facility in many situations – these were qualities valued by those

who gave him commissions. Not seldom the completion of commissions had to be rushed, and Henrici reported proudly: "Quite often I felt like a mail courier, I had to bridle Pegasus in the middle of the night, even when no inspiration seemed to respond." As contemporaries remarked, his poetic skill was soon so practiced that "not only did it provide him with sustenance, but it gave him real fulfillment." In 1727, he became "Actuarius" for the mail service, then "Secretarius", and finally "Commissarius" for the whole system. In 1740 he received authority to collect county taxes and the Leipzig civic beverage tax connected with the wine inspection, "for all of which his status as a poet had recommended him well." Of frail and weakly stature, and married to an ever-ailing wife, he had proved enough energy and endurance to rise from the lowest academic level to a respected position.

Evidently he knew quite a bit about music, and it seems that he played in one of the two Leipzig collegia musica, possibly the one conducted by Bach. A passage in a wedding poem of 1730 provides a hint:

In thinking of courtship,
One will do well to join a collegium musicum.
Going to one's [music] desk
And finding one's part,
One turns the pages
To see if it is difficult to play.
Like that, one has first
To probe the maiden, in a general way
To see how she feels in her heart.

Picander's collaboration with Bach can be traced from 1725 to the 1740s; the St. Thomas cantor is known to have put more than thirty of his texts to music – the "Peasant Cantata", the "Streit zwischen Phoebus und Pan", the "Aeolus Cantata", "Herkules am Scheidewege", and a number of sacred cantatas. His most well known libretto (perhaps also his best) is that for the *St. Matthew Passion.*

Picander's *Ernst-Schertzhaffte und Satyrische Gedichte*, which appeared in five volumes, largely re-issued, were the result of many years of work. Those that are "ernsthaft" (mostly odes of mourning and sacred texts) do not form a very large segment; prevailing are rhymed wedding offerings, replete with unambiguous touches. This provoked massive criticism by contemporaries, especially Gottsched and his circle, without, however, altering Picander's favorable reception by the public. Consideration for his customers is evident in satires on common themes that – in the words of his biographer – were not intended for [moral] betterment so much as for sale. This may also apply to the following text of 1727, based on some occurrence in France, but aimed at Leipzig:

A royal court order was posted at the parliament.
It said: we have for some time and most unfortunately sensed
That many a person is driven to ruin by coffee.
In order to preclude such calamity in time
No one may [herewith] venture to drink coffee,
Except the King and his court,
Others will be prohibited,
Though permission may be granted on occasion…
At this there was much wailing.
Ah, cried the women, rather take our bread.
For without coffee our life will expire.
What else could we have in the morning
Since we have to abandon our wont?
How sadly shall we reminisce

That those were good days,
When my friends and I sat together,
Drinking some coffee as we played cards.
Yet the king's mind was not to be changed,
And people soon perished like flies,
To be buried in vast numbers as in a time of plague.
And womenfolk dwindled appallingly,
Until the order was revoked and destroyed,
And extinction subsided in France.

This life-threatening development came at a time when Paris had 380 coffee houses, with a special clientele for each: literary people, music friends, actors, officers, opera singers, merchants – but also those flighty damsels whose trade is supposed to

be the oldest in history. As early as 1690 the coffee trade had grown to such an extent that the Crown – true to the principles of a business-oriented economy – could sell a coffee monopoly to a general leaseholder. Since the King, in his never-ending financial difficulties (court decor and war used up enormous sums), soon decided on a higher price (thus crushing the lease arrangement), there arose a "coffee crisis" which Picander rekindled in his doggerel of 1727.

Five years later, he published, at the end of Part Three of his *Ernst-Schertzhaffte und Satyrische Gedichte*, the text for a coffee cantata. Possibly this was a reprint of an earlier text, perhaps even set to music previously – but, if so, not by Bach. Not before 1734 did Bach decide on his composition – whether prompted by particular circumstances, by the urging of friends, or because he was irked by the superficial manner this text had been treated and wanted to show that it had more possibilities – all this can no longer be ascertained.

The St. Thomas Cantor at Fifty

At this time Bach was in his fiftieth year, married
for the second time, and of his seventeen children
born to this point – seven from the first marriage, and ten from the second – seven had sur-vi-
ved. Wilhelm Friedemann, the oldest son,
was organist at the newest and most beautiful
Silbermann organ in the Saxon domain since
June 1733. The second son, Carl Philipp
Emanuel, was about to take up the study of law
in Frankfurt an der Oder. A few years earlier the
St. Thomas cantor had proudly reported to his
boyhood friend, Georg Erdmann in Danzig, that
his children were born musicians, so that with his
family he could produce a whole concert "voca-
liter und instrumentaliter".

In a little more than three decades of creative activity, an oeuvre had arisen which – so far as can be determined today – included more than 200 church cantatas, Passion settings according to John, Matthew, and Mark, a large number of secular cantatas, works of Latin sacred music, among which was a Missa in B minor presented to the Saxon Elector with the appeal for the granting of a court title (the success of which required waiting), as well as an abundance of instrumental music for organ, harpsichord, and large and small ensembles. Planned for the end of 1734 was a large oratorio comprising a sequence of cantatas for the feast days from Christmas to Epiphany.

Sheer ability, industry, and perseverance had allotted a certain affluence to the St. Thomas cantor, to which the estate listing after his death in 1750 attests. Next to books, instruments, clothing, and monetary funds, some household articles are listed, such as table silver and other valuables, one large coffeepot worth 19 Thaler and 12 Groschen, also several smaller ones worth 10 Thaler and 20 Groschen, one coffee-plate worth 5 Thaler and 12 Groschen, a copper and brass coffeepot, also one small one and one smaller yet.

It remains a conjecture whether these household objects justify the assumption that the habit of coffee drinking occasionally might have been excessive even in the Bach family. If so, the St. Thomas cantor's coffee cantata might have been a bit of a "*sinfonia domestica*".

Johann Sebastian Bach had concertized regularly with his collegium musicum in public for more than ten years: from spring 1729 until the beginning of the forties, with an interruption from spring 1737 to fall 1739. One can hardly interpret this fact otherwise than that it signified an important enlargement of the cantorship at St. Thomas's toward the function of a civic music director.

To what extent the circumstances were commensurate with the composer's ability is a different question. We can assume, on the basis of the evening rehearsal times alone (which as far as possible avoided overlap with the usual coffeehouse bustle) that the public concerts of the collegia musica were not anything like "elevated coffeehouse music". The functions of the cafétier – until 1741 Gottfried Zimmermann, then Enoch Richter – were restricted to the offer of a venue and the sale of refreshments to participants and audience. Any rules and regulations for visitors are unfortunately wanting, but what has been preserved in a 1735 "arrangement" for the collegium in neighboring Delitzsch – apparently modeled after the Leipzig organization – may have applied also in Leipzig:

"[…] 6. Those auditors who would like to smoke tobacco, passing the time to greater advantage, may have pipe and tobacco carried to the collegium by their servants. 7. Gentlemen in the audience will remember without special admonition that it will behoove them to avoid playing cards or pursuing other pleasures that may disturb the collegium."

So far as smoking and playing cards were concerned, even if "what behooved" could be arranged
with the establishment of appropriate rules, a
much larger problem remained, which apparently
all those giving concerts in the eighteenth century were not (or only under great difficulty) able to
face. Experiences of the kind were had in 1771 in
Leipzig by Johann Friedrich Reichardt, at that
time nineteen years old, when he visited the
"Grosse Concert", the early form of the Gewand-
haus concerts, which had followed the collegia by
that time.

He entered "a brightly lit auditorium filled
with gallant society, which was perhaps a little
more heavily powdered, sitting more stiffly, and
debating the music more unashamedly than one
finds in other concerts, but having in common
with audiences everywhere a penchant for loud
conversation and noise. It is true, a manager re-
sponsible for the concert keeps watch and, when
some people talk all too loudly, knocks a large
key of the building against the clavecin (which
he thus puts out of tune), and asks them for
silence though it is not kept. His courageous
interference is limited to the gentlemen. For the

ladies he reserves a courtesy learned in Paris by joining them in their discourse."

Regional differences in this respect were reported in 1794 by a Berlin music journal. Its correspondent praised the Halle students for being very well behaved and attentive as concert visitors – or at least they had been so in former years:

"In Göttingen I found an unusual amount of misbehavior during concerts; the babbling of young beaus and the idle talk of damsels beleaguered by dandies often veritably blotted out the music. And it pervaded as if the spawning time of frogs had occasioned a new generation."

Bleak experiences were "gathered" at about the same time by a visitor of a brilliant court musical, in which great virtuosos "presented a Quadro most delectably". Yet the company took no notice and continued conversing and gambling with undiminished clamor. Finally, our music lover, who was also an accomplished draftsman, lost his patience: "By God", he commenced, casting a savage glance like lightning over the audience, "when I draw a picture of a concert hall, I will draw all the people without ears, and the lonely virtuoso playing before the assembly with very long ears."

Such was the report in the *Journal des Luxus und der Moden*. Any remedies were hard, if not impossible, to find. At Mozart's time in Vienna, it was the authority of the Baron van Swieten that served to turn off all conversation during a performance:

"For even when a whispering exchange should arise, His Excellency, who used to sit in one of the front rows, used to rise in his full length, with solemn dignity, turn to the guilty ones, giving them a weighty look, and sat down again. This had the desired effect every time."

The Drama's First Act

"In Zimmermann's coffee house" or in the adjoining garden "at the Grimmische Gateway", wherever the original performance of Bach's coffee cantata may have been, there was surely no available excellency that could restore order and attention. Thus Picander – and with him, Bach – placed at the head of the cantata (which is actually intended to be a dialogue) a protagonist, in the following quite superfluous, a blend of narrator and huckster.

Be silent, talk not,
And listen to what is happening.
Herr Schlendrian now appears
With his daughter Liesgen,

Growling like a bear.
Hear for yourselves what she did to him:

In an opera libretto, it would now read: "Enter Schlendrian and Liesgen" but Picander and Bach say nothing about the question of scenic action. Bach's designation "Drama per Musica" does admit an association with Gottsched's *Versuch einer critischen Dichtkunst* (1730), which concedes the attribute "drama" to such cantatas "as might be performed or acted by real personages." By way of restriction and in ambiguous manner, however, Gottsched continues: "While such dramata are rarely sung on stage but rather in a room, with the singers not appearing in appropriate costume, the texts must still be so arranged that a performance in action would be possible."

One could indeed act out the coffee cantata. But attempts of the kind have only shown that neither text nor music benefit by it. Scenery and action are implied in abundance. But if a stage director were to avoid encumbrances that disturb the nature of the work, he would have to limit himself to most sparing suggestions. A few harp-sichord arpeggios – "con pompa" – and Schlendrian's entrance is sufficiently sketched. His aria, with its exposition of some basic educational wisdom, is designed merely to project his rumbling and blustering temperament and his frustration at "today's youth", interested only in new-fangled things and dismissing the experience of their elders.

Does one not have a hundred thousand troubles with one's children!
What I say day after day
To my daughter Liesgen
Bears no fruit at all.

Grumbling figures ascending in the violin and accompanying bass; large melodic skips, angular motion – those are Bach's means to portray an angry father trying in vain to contain himself. Tone repetitions, grim and resolute in the major key, lamenting and desperate in the minor key, mirror the daily installment of family pedagogy in its intention and success. Up to this point the theme of coffee has not appeared – now it does:

SCHLENDRIAN:
You naughty child, disobedient daughter,
Oh, when will I get my wish
That you give up coffee.

LIESGEN:
Father, sir, do not be so rough.
If I cannot have my cup of coffee three times a day,
I will become, to my dismay,
Like a shriveled-up nanny-goat steak.

This is only an initial skirmish: emotions rise only a little, the arguments derived from the arsenal of every-day use. If the father's part (the exclamation "Oh") modulates to F-sharp major, it is mere exaggeration, as is the comparison with the dried-up goat meat.

Also a little overdone, doubtless, is Liesgen's hymn to the brown beverage:

Ey! How sweet the coffee tastes
Sweeter than a thousand kisses,
Milder than a muscatel.
Coffee, coffee, I must have.
If you want to enchant me,
Give me some coffee.

In moderate dancing motion, rather like a minuet, and in the key of B minor, which was reserved for highest sentiment, the voice of the coffee-struck girl rises, vying in airy garlands with the flute, the classical attribute of sweetness, loveliness and pleasurableness. Then it mounts to a combative attitude ("Coffee I must have") and sinks down again in longing syncopation and languishing fermatas. Even without knowing the "appropriate costume" we can imagine a figure something like Liotard's "chocolate girl" painted in 1743. Who might it have been who sang this susceptive aria in 1734?

More easily answered than this question is the one concerning the identity of the protagonist Schlendrian. According to all we know, it might have been the Johann Christian Hoffmann who in November 1734, a few weeks after the performance of the coffee cantata, applied for a teaching post in Plauen and remarked that for four years "he had assisted Herr Capell-Meister Bach's church music as a bassist, and had been so fortunate as to sing in an evening music before His Royal Highness, the Majesty of Poland, receiving his approbation." The cantata performed in the presence of the Saxon Elector was "Preise dein Glücke, gesegnetes Sachsen"; the war-like bass aria, "Rase nur, verwegner Schwarm", called for the highest vocal qualifications. His vocal abilities would therefore have been quite sufficient for the coffee cantata; the question is whether Hoffmann, then about twenty-five years of age, had the physique to render the role of the father convincingly.

There are several candidates for the flute part in Liesgen's hymn to coffee, for after some initial difficulties the transverse flute had become quite fashionable in Leipzig. One might think, for instance, of Jacob von Stählin from Memmingen in

Swabia, who was a student in Leipzig and later active as a diplomat in Russia, a friend of the Bach family. Or the third son of the St. Thomas cantor, Johann Gottfried Bernhard; his nickname "the windy", however, poses some doubt regarding his reliability.

The harpsichord part may have been taken by Bach's second-oldest son, Carl Philipp Emanuel, perhaps as a farewell performance before his departure for the Viadrina, the University of Frankfurt an der Oder.

There remains the issue of the solo soprano. A participation of female singers at the collegium was totally out of the question. Fifty years later Johann Adam Hiller, the later St. Thomas cantor and Bach's third successor, reported in retrospect that there were "never other singers, but that a violist or violinist stepped up to take, with screeching falsetto voice, the aria part of Salinbeni, which, furthermore, he could not read very well." Hiller, who said at another occasion that coffee houses "had long been the asylum of music in Leipzig" spoke from his own experience. Yet since he was the one who got female singers to the Leipzig concert stage, his negative judgment about falsetto singing may not have to be taken too literally.

In a novel published in 1700 about a musician written by Bach's Leipzig predecessor, Johann Kuhnau, there is a remark about a singer: "when he played the harpsichord and let his alto-falsettino be heard in some love songs (his normal voice was bass), the maiden was quite taken in." A Leipzig concert report from 1743 mentions the Eisenach court singer Voigt, a bass "who not only had a fine deep bass but also, in two arias, an incomparable alto voice." In 1752, an alumnus of the Schweinfurt Gymnasium is attested of "having accomplished the musical feat of singing commendably in treble, tenor, and bass voice" (Philipp Spitta, the great Bach biographer, observed that "this praise surely refers to being versed in reading different clefs." Writing in 1873, he evidently had no knowledge of the artistic usage of the falsetto register – its significance had probably quite disappeared in the nineteenth century.) The role of Liesgen in the Leipzig collegium musicum must therefore be understood in terms of this somewhat sparse and sharp-edged vocal production, probably by a student. We do not know whether, with costume and makeup, he might have tried to buttress the illusion of a girl. The period evidently did not take any exception to this situation, just as today there is no objection to the role of Oktavian in "Rosenkavalier".

The argument between father and daughter presented was thus actually one between two students discussing home or "law and order" problems:

SCHLENDRIAN:
If you don't give up coffee,
You shall not attend any wedding feasts
Or take any pleasure walks.

LIESGEN:
All right. But let me have my coffee!

SCHLENDRIAN:
There goes the little monkey!
I shall not get you
That fashionably wide whalebone skirt.

LIESGEN:
I can easily give that up.

SCHLENDRIAN:
You will not be allowed to stand by the window
to watch the passers-by.

LIESGEN:
That will be all right, too.
Only leave me with coffee.

SCHLENDRIAN:
You will not have the silver or gold braid
For your bonnet.

LIESGEN:
All well – just let me have my pleasure.

SCHLENDRIAN:
You naughty Liesgen
You will give up everything else?

A musical and literary model for this contest of rebuttals is found in the contemporaneous comic opera intermezzo; for instance, in Georg Philipp Telemann's "Die Ungleiche Heyrath/Oder das Herrschsüchtige Cammer-Mädgen" of 1725. Here the damsel's wishes are similarly debated. The elderly rich Pimpinone wants to test his

chambermaid, and she seems to give in to everything. Between them the following dialogue deve-
lops:

All right! Let's come to a conclusion!
Long dalliance is disagreeable to my mind.
   I agree with that.
Do you like to watch from the window?
   I don't like it at all.
Visit the opera and ballet?
   I never do.
Like a card game?
   Privacy is my pleasure.
Do you like to read novels?
   I prefer my almanacs.
Do you enjoy a masquerade?
   I would rather sit in the kitchen.
Or a bear and oxen fight?
   My choice is to stay at home.
Good. Then you shall be my dear wife.

Needless to say, afterwards everything is quite different. In the *Coffee Cantata*, Schlendrian is at first
undecided. The recitative ends with a question and
concludes musically with a Phrygian cadence – as
in the center of Brandenburg Concertos Nos. 3

and 4. He is taken to pondering. His E-minor aria is marked by a theme that is closely chromatic.

Maidens of a strong mind
Are hard to sway.
Yet if you touch the right spot,
You will succeed.

The theme on which this aria is built passes through all half-steps of the chromatic scale within six measures. It is a type of theme that can mean chagrin, pain, grief, or – to speak in terms borrowed from Bach's student Kirnberger – furnishes a model for expressing the utmost desperation. Doubtless, such is the state of mind into which Schlendrian has gotten himself. The numerous sighing suspensions vividly stress the worries of the pained father; the strong interval thrusts correspond to the "maiden's strong mind". The unwieldy theme resulted in some headache even to the composer, causing vigorous corrections in his composing copy. The word "maiden", exclaimed three times in ascending range, as Schlendrian is about to resume the aria theme, suggests – to quote Johann Kuhnau – "the manner of unsure singers, probing for their tones in a vacillating way." It reflects ultimate confusion.

Then – "touching the right spot" – comes an inspiration that saves the case: chromaticism seems to disappear but, like the sinister Doktor Mirakel in Jacques Offenbach's opera "Hoffmann's Erzählungen" – returns from the other side. Nevertheless, the "spot" has been found. Joyful coloraturas form a counterpoint to the desperate chromatic theme. A last soft "if you touch the right spot" appears, like a contented rubbing of hands for the anticipated triumph.

With pretended equanimity, like the cat slinking stealthily around the hot dish, Schlendrian approaches the argument from another side. The bland key of C major assists his coup de grâce.

SCHLENDRIAN:
Now listen to what your father is saying.

LIESGEN:
Always, except about coffee.

SCHLENDRIAN:
All right, you will have to acquiesce
To never taking a husband.

LIESGEN:
Father, sir, no husband?

SCHLENDRIAN:
I swear – you shall have none.

LIESGEN:
Until I give up coffee?
Then, coffee, farewell!
Father, I will not touch it evermore.

SCHLENDRIAN:
So you will finally have your man.

Now the magic formula has been spoken. The "unsuspecting angel" is overjoyed.

Today, dear father, today!
Oh, a man!
Indeed, that will be to my liking.
If only it did come about
That, lastly, rather than coffee,
Before I go to bed,
I will have a fine lover.

Liesgen's aria, in its swiftly-moving 6/8-rhythm, its persuasive melody, and its warm string accompaniment, reveals the exuberant and sincere joy of the girl. The instruments' constant motion, especially in the obbligato harpsichord part, is a picture of her tantalizing impatience. And various drags and scrolls, as well as the syncopating "Lombard gusto" lend a fashionable quality to the aria. Yet the music has a double character: the modish touches may also bear out the volatile nature of the young girl; the basic pulse, somewhat like a siciliano, tends toward the gigue; and the many G-major cadences returning to the basic key describe (according to the Hamburg theorist Johann Mattheson) a "homespun yearning". The fact that the instruments play *piano* precisely when Liesgen

utters the somewhat indelicate "before I go to bed" is a delightful discourtesy of the composer.

To Picander's mind, this was a fitting end to the story, and some of his fellow composers followed him in this idea. Not so, Bach. He "topples" the play, as one might say, in a gamboling way. He summons the narrator again out of his absence and lets him comment:

Now old Schlendrian goes to see
How he can promptly get a husband
For his daughter Liesgen.
But Liesgen spreads the rumor
"No suitor need apply
Without a promise,
Written into the marriage contract,
That I will be allowed
To have my coffee whenever I wish."

This text appears in the score in Bach's most careful penmanship – more careful than in the case of any of his other recitative texts (which, in principle, were written more carefully than texts in arias or choruses to begin with). Perhaps this was meant to be a help for writing out parts or printing the text for the audience. If so, it would lend strength to the notion that the text addition was Bach's own. The same might apply to the final lines:

Women will hold to their coffee.
Mother likes coffee,
So does grandmother.
Who, in the end would berate the daughters!

This somewhat lengthy coda, a song-like terzetto with the accompaniment of all instruments is close to the dance character of the bourée and, with its unusual three-measure groupings, rather defies convention. With the capricious figures of the obbligato flute part it finally recalls Liesgen's hymn to her favorite beverage. Thus all ends well – at least in Bach's cantata.

Epilogue

Yet, coffee was still to experience its true odyssey. The custom of drinking coffee, spreading as it did to all parts of the populace, began to reduce the consumption of inland-produced beer (and the beer tax), while the fiscal authorities for German princes and dukes watched the financial drain resulting from coffee imports with growing unease. An increase of the tax rate, ordered in Prussia, was of little help since there arose extensive smuggling of coffee. State authorities tried to counter this by ordering that legally imported coffee could be roasted only in official establishments. Forbidden private roasting was to be prevented by inaugurating a veritable army of "coffee sniffers". Soldiers discharged from the armed services carried out this mission for years throughout the country, until in 1787 the restriction was finally revoked.

A Hessen-Cassel edict of January 28, 1766, saw resolute measures to curb the devastating excess of the use of coffee. It stipulated that:

"1) Coffee dealers were no longer permitted in the country, and coffee could no longer be sold; all supply had to be abandoned within three months under threat of punishment and confiscation. 2) Peasants, laborers, and service people were to abstain completely under threat of a 10-Thaler fine or 14-day prison sentence. 3) If they owned any coffee accessories they had to dispose of them within six weeks [...]. 4) In cities, respected and well-to-do citizens were still to be permitted to drink coffee. Yet 5) less affluent citizens were to be sharply observed, warned about the rather destructive nature of coffee, and duly punished in cases of abuse. 6) But workers and all service people, wasting their time on the vice of drinking coffee, were totally forbidden its use under threat of punishment as noted above."

An even more rigorous note was struck by a 1780 order emanating from the Bishop of Hildesheim:

"German men! Your fathers drank liquor; like Frederick the Great, they were brought up on beer, and their spirit was high. We should do likewise. Let us deliver wood and wine to the wealthy half-brothers of the German nation, but no longer funds for coffee. All pots, fancy and plain cups, coffee mills, roasting devices, thus all that can be associated with coffee, shall be crushed and demolished, so any recollection of it among our fellow-citizens will be destroyed. Those who would dare to sell its beans will have their whole supply confiscated, and anyone acquiring accessories to consume it will be locked up."

The situation in England was described by Leopold Mozart in his letter of May 28, 1764 from London:

"Because beer is a *productum* of this country [England], wine is incredibly expensive, with an enormous tax. The same is true of coffee, which is more than 4 German *Gulden* a pound. What's more, one must buy it already roasted and milled, which is done in special places. If you roast a pound of coffee at home, you will be fined fifty guineas. Imagine the face my wife made at these arrangements. Well then – the English market their tea, and prevent their money from going abroad for coffee."

All of this belongs already to a time of little understanding for Bach's vocal music, including his "comic cantatas". The coffee cantata was not resurrected until 1837 when it appeared in print, almost a century after its presumably last performance during Bach's life. At that time the *Frankfurter Nachrichten* had reported:

"On Tuesday, April 7, a musicus from out-of-town will give a concert in the Kauffhauss unter den neuen Krämen. Among other things, a music drama of Schlendrian with his daughter Liesgen will be performed."

This happened in the year 1739. Ten years later, a few streets down, was born a certain Johann

Wolfgang Goethe, who, at the age of sixteen, came to Leipzig, to the cake baker Hendel – but we've already been through that. Only *Kuchengartenstrasse* remains in the eastern outskirts of Leipzig as a witness of former splendor. The "Coffee tree", however, has weathered all hazards and risen to new bloom. A visit there will be well worth it, for the 300-year-tradition alone. And the successors of "Lehmann's widow" will surely welcome any inquiry for a "mocca double".

And – one never knows – perhaps, by pure coincidence, a performance of Johann Sebastian Bach's *Coffee Cantata* will be taking place just then at the near-by Old City Hall or some other historic location. Including this in one's visit would be recommended as well, but one would have to listen rather judiciously – there are a few things about it …

Richter Kaffee
gegr. Leipzig 1879

This book is accompanied by a recording of the Coffee Cantata on CD. It is part of the composite recording of all the cantatas by Johann Sebastian Bach (Erato/Challenge Classics). We are grateful to Ton Koopman for providing the material.